Foreword by Patrick Fitzgerald

TAKING BACK THE LAND

From Containment To Victory

PAMELA A. SEGNERI

Taking Back The Land - From Containment To Victory

Copyright © 2024 - Pamela Segneri

All rights reserved. This book is protected by the copyright laws of Australia. This book may not be copied or reprinted for commercial gain or profit. The use of short quotations or occasional page copying for personal or group study is permitted and encouraged provided the source is acknowledged. Permission will be granted upon request. Unless otherwise identified, Scripture quotations are taken from the New American Standard Bible® NASB® Copyright © 1960, 1971, 1977, 1995, 2020 by The Lockman Foundation. Used by permission. All rights reserved. www.Lockman.org. Scripture quotations marked TPT are from The Passion Translation®. Copyright © 2017 by BroadStreet Publishing® Group, LLC. Used by permission. All rights reserved. thePassionTranslation.com. Scripture quotations marked NKJV are from The Holy Bible, New King James Version. Copyright © 1982 by Thomas Nelson, Inc. Used by permission. All rights reserved. www.thenkjvbible.com. Emphasis with Scripture quotations is the author's own. Please note that Mountain Train Media's publishing style capitalizes certain pronouns in Scripture that refer to the Father, Son, and Holy Spirit, and may differ from some Bible publishers' styles. Take note that the name satan and related names are not capitalized. We choose not to acknowledge him, even to the point of violating grammatical rules.

Published by Mountain Train Media
QLD, Australia
publishing@mountaintrainmedia.com.au
www.mountaintrainmedia.com.au

ISBN: 978-0-6453782-6-9

Dedication

This is of course for the Lord Jesus Christ without whom I would have no idea of how to take back the land.

To my precious family;

Paul, my husband without whom I wouldn't be where I am today. His belief in me and unconditional love for me is astounding. To my sons and their families - this is the legacy the Lord is building.

To each one of you as you read these words, I pray the Lord is strengthening you to stand and see victory manifesting in your lives. I decree Shalom - nothing broken, nothing missing!

4 TAKING BACK THE LAND

Acknowledgements

As with any project there have been many who have encouraged and assisted along the way. First and foremost I acknowledge that without the inspiartion and guidance of Holy Spirit this work would never have existed.

I want to especially acknowledge the tireless work of my husband Paul, his editing and design skills have been a gift.

The incredible encouragement I have experienced along the way from my dear friend Barb Krueger.

I also want to recognise the gift of encouragement both Patrick Fitzgerald and Bruce Lindley are to me with their very kind words in the forward and introduction respectively. To read their endorsements is incredibly humbling as these Apostolic fathers in the Faith actually get me!

6 TAKING BACK THE LAND

Contents

Foreword: Patrick Fitzgerald....p9

Introduction....p11

Preface....p15

Chapter 1: He Trains My Hands For War, My Fingers For Battle....p17

Chapter 2: It's Time To Conquer....p27

Chapter 3: Occupying The Land....p41

Chapter 4: Giants In The Land....p45

Chapter 5: The Hittites....p51

Chapter 6: The Amorites....p55

Chapter 7: The Canaanites....p59

Chapter 8: The Hivites....p63

Chapter 9: The Girgashites....p69

Chapter 10: The Perizzites....p75

Chapter 11: The Jebusites....p81

Chapter 12: The Last Word....p87

Foreword

"Taking Back the Land", what a title, what a message for the days we live in! This amazing new book by Pamela Segneri is, in my opinion, an anointed message for 'such a time as this'.

Pamela's insight into the authority and position of the believer is not only informative but prophetic as it calls us to stand, believe, conquer and reclaim the land in the days we live. At times claiming the promises of God requires courage, faith, and determination.

Reflecting on the journey of the children of Israel as they pursued God's promises Pamela draws inspiration and insight from their experiences, highs and lows, building faith in the believer, instilling an assurance that the land is ours, promised by God, despite disappointment and discouragement at times.

We live in a time when it is imperative that believers stand in the authority that is theirs through Christ. Many walk in inferiority when the sacrifice of Christ, once and for all, assures us that the victory is ours. I firmly believe that there is a cry from heaven in these days, calling us to stand in the authority of Christ, walking in His victory, living in the land that He has promised.

Pamela's book is not only timely, but it is an absolute weapon in the hand of the believer who will stand and walk as more than a conqueror. As you read these pages I encourage you to open your heart, search deep within and find the courage, faith and determination that is within you to believe, achieve and fulfil in the promised land of God.

> *"Yet in all these things we are more than conquerors through Him who loved us."*
> Romans 8:37 NKJV

Patrick Fitzgerald
Senior Pastor
People's Church Dublin

Introduction

"Taking Back the Land" by Pamela Segneri is not just a normal book. It is written from years of application of powerful, practical, biblical principles. So much so that it has become Pamela's lifestyle of breakthrough and victory. It can be yours too!

God is the ultimate promise-keeper. As faithful and present as He was for Joshua so He is with you. In Joshua 1, God told Joshua three times to be "Be strong and courageous." It is time for you to rise up and apply that in your life too.

Pamela is right. We are not just meant to overcome and conquer life's obstacles; we are destined by God to live there. To occupy those strongholds permanently. God intends you to rule! Like Joshua God's destiny for you is that "No one is able to stand against you all the days of your life."

Not only will "Taking Back the Land" inspire you, it will teach you how to deal with the different "giants" of obstacles that come to us all in life.

Get ready, you are about to be challenged, equipped, and receive boldness. It is time for you to rise up and "take back YOUR land" like you have never done before!

Bruce Lindley
Lead Apostle
ARC Global Apostolic Community

Preface

We often talk of the Great Harvest however, if we wind that back a little each of us must be prepared, equipped, armed and dangerous.

We are all called by Jesus to fulfil a role and regardless of where you may see yourself, you are a leader in whatever sphere of influence you operate in and make no mistake, God called you and He needs each of us to fulfil our destiny.

Right now our destiny is to recognise what has been stolen. Which part of our inheritance has the enemy moved into and pushed us out of?

You may be surprised that it is more than you thought. Jesus already won the victory and it is ours today.

My prayer is that after reading this book, you are re-fired and equipped for the days ahead.

CHAPTER 1

He Trains My Hands For War My Fingers For Battle

Firstly we have to claim it!

What is it that you have had stolen? You need to know this in order to claim its return. This could be family, friends, finance, business, ministry, promotion, inheritance, peace, love. These are just a few, what is it for you?

It is God's desire that we would be victorious on the earth. That's why Jesus came!

We must walk according to what God says and not what the world says. Have you ever noticed what the world cites as fact today will be different tomorrow? And yet the truth is God's Word never changes. As we walk according to God's Word, that is Abundant Life!

Joshua 1 - This word is for me and each one of us.

Now it came about after the death of Moses the servant of the LORD, that the LORD spoke to Joshua the son of Nun, Moses' servant, saying, "Moses My servant is dead; so now arise, cross this Jordan, you and all this people, to the land which I am giving to them, to the sons of Israel. Every place on which the sole of your foot steps, I have given it to you, just as I spoke to Moses. From the wilderness and this Lebanon, even as far as the great river, the river Euphrates, all the land of the Hittites, and as far as the Great Sea toward the setting of the sun will be your territory. No one will be able to oppose you all the days of your life. Just as I have been with Moses, I will be with you; I will not desert you nor abandon you. Be strong and courageous, for you shall give this people possession of the land which I swore to their fathers to give them. Only be strong and very courageous; be careful to do according to all the Law which Moses My servant commanded you; do not turn from it to the right or to the left, so that you may achieve success wherever you go. This Book of the Law shall not depart from your mouth, but you shall meditate on it day and night, so that you may be careful to do according to all that is written in it; for then you will make your way prosperous, and then you will achieve success. Have I not commanded you? Be strong and courageous! Do not be terrified nor dismayed, for the LORD your God is with you wherever you go." Then Joshua commanded the officers of the people, saying, "Pass through the midst of the camp and command the people, saying, 'Prepare provisions for yourselves, for within three days you are going to cross this Jordan, to go in to take possession of the land which the LORD your God is giving you, to possess it.'" But to the Reubenites, to the Gadites, and to the half-tribe of Manasseh, Joshua said, "Remember the word which Moses the servant of the LORD commanded you, saying, 'The LORD your God is giving you rest, and will give you this land.' Your wives, your little ones, and your livestock shall remain in the land which Moses gave you beyond the Jordan, but you shall cross ahead of your brothers in battle formation, all your valiant warriors, and shall help them, until the LORD gives your brothers rest, as He is giving you, and they also possess the land which the LORD your God is giving them. Then you may return to your own land, and take possession of that which Moses the servant of the LORD gave you beyond the Jordan toward the sunrise." They answered Joshua, saying, "All that you have commanded us we will do, and wherever you send us we will go. Just as we obeyed Moses in all things, so we will obey you; only may the LORD your God be with you as He was with Moses. Anyone who rebels against your command and does not obey your words in all that you command him, shall be put to death; only be strong and courageous." Joshua 1:1-18 NASB2020

There are seven promises that God gives to Joshua in this passage. I read them as God is promising me!

1. You will possess vast territory (v3-4)

2. No one will be able to defeat you (v5)

3. God will be with you as He was with Moses (v5)

4. God will never fail you (v5)

5. God will never abandon you (v5)

6. You will enjoy prosperity and success (v8)

7. God will be with you wherever you go (v9)

We can take them as ours as they are fulfilled in Jesus in whom we are included for receiving all of God's promises as YES and AMEN.

Let's just back track a little.

Now in order to claim our land it is paramount that we know who we are in Christ. Our identity and our knowledge of that identity must be unassailable. That shows the enemy who we are and we refuse to be moved from that position of being seated in heavenly places with Jesus. We are above only and not beneath!

We must get the truth of who we are in Christ into our spirit and deep within every cell of our body. When we know the truth that will indeed set us free! Until we do we may say the words but will truly be claiming nothing. Sort of I am saying this because everyone else is and I just hope it will work although it didn't last time etc etc….

Through that kind of thinking, we have allowed the enemy to come in to claim what was promised to us.

In Genesis 2, God placed Adam in the garden and gave him dominion. That is…. Authority to rule! God wants us to rule with that authority. We can only do that when there is no doubt in us about who we are in Him.

Sometimes we may be really good in most spheres of life yet there maybe one or two dark areas which have been closed off to the light of God. Perhaps because we may feel shame if they were brought into the light.

God already knows and Jesus did not come to shame us - He came to set us free!

There are other parts of us that are locked down due to no action of our own. Suffice to say these are not your fault and you may not have any conscious knowledge of them. They are generational curses and this may be the land you are taking back.

There were certain things that seemed to hound me in my youth even though I loved the Lord and functioned in ministry. I randomly discovered as my Mum was going through some old papers that my paternal Grandfather and great Grandfather had been heavily involved in Freemasonry. This was shocking to me! As I looked for help asking the question, "How do I get set free?", it seemed to me I was exchanging one bondage for another. There were those who on finding this out wanted to shame me; which was not helpful. One person even told me I could never be free of it and that's when the Spirit of the Lord raised up a standard over me. He miraculously set me free and cut it off my bloodline. I believed He could and He did!

His love is greater than any other force as we yield to Him completely. He wants us to rule with His authority!

Moving on, satan calls into question the promises of God. 'Did God really say…?' That's satan's playbook, that's the way every demon/principality tries to get you. They are the voices of confusion that we've pretty much all heard however, when we hear them we must shut them down. Don't give them your time.

It's time to take back what was given to us!

We often hear, 'Why are others blessed and not me?'

We're going to deal with that here in this book.

The promises of God given to Abram were fulfilled in Christ. They are yes and in Him AMEN!

> *Now the LORD said to Abram, "Go from your country, And from your relatives And from your father's house, To the land which I will show you; And I will make you into a great nation, And I will bless you, And make your name great; And you shall be a blessing; And I will bless those who bless you, And the one who curses you I will curse. And in you all the families of the earth will be blessed." Genesis 12:1-3* NASB2020

Let's look at Numbers 13:25-33

> *When they returned from spying out the land, at the end of forty days, they went on and came to Moses and Aaron and to all the congregation of the sons of Israel, in the wilderness of Paran at Kadesh; and they brought back word to them*

and to all the congregation, and showed them the fruit of the land. So they reported to him and said, "We came into the land where you sent us, and it certainly does flow with milk and honey, and this is its fruit. Nevertheless, the people who live in the land are strong, and the cities are fortified and very large. And indeed, we saw the descendants of Anak there! Amalek is living in the land of the Negev, the Hittites, the Jebusites, and the Amorites are living in the hill country, and the Canaanites are living by the sea and by the side of the Jordan." Then Caleb quieted the people before Moses and said, "We should by all means go up and take possession of it, for we will certainly prevail over it." But the men who had gone up with him said, "We are not able to go up against the people, because they are too strong for us." So they brought a bad report of the land which they had spied out to the sons of Israel, saying, "The land through which we have gone to spy out is a land that devours its inhabitants; and all the people whom we saw in it are people of great stature. We also saw the Nephilim there (the sons of Anak are part of the Nephilim); and we were like grasshoppers in our own sight, and so we were in their sight."*
Numbers 13:25-33 NASB2020

With that in mind, who are we? Do we listen to the

voice of reason or do we listen to the voice of FAITH and just believe!

In Joshua 1:2, God encourages Joshua and therefore us to 'Get up and go'! To claim our land we must get up.

> "Moses My servant is dead; so now arise, cross this Jordan, you and all this people, to the land which I am giving to them, to the sons of Israel. Joshua 1:2 NASB2020

God wants us to claim the promise so we must change our posture.

Whatever we have been doing isn't working therefore we need to change it, this is not simply change for the sake of change.

God is excited when we begin to claim what has been stolen but His greater desire is for us to conquer.

CHAPTER 2

It's Time To Conquer

In order to conquer we need a mindset shift. Every victory is first won in our mind. The mind is the devils playground we cannot entertain him.

In Numbers 13, Moses sent out twelve spies as the Lord had instructed him, one from each of the tribes of Israel.

From verse 25, after 40 days the spies returned. The report that ten of them gave showed they were already defeated in their minds. Although the land was certainly a land of abundance, they were overwhelmed by the people who occupied the land. They were ferocious, they lived in fortified cities and incidentally they were giants.

These guys were beaten before they began. They were beaten not because of the opposition rather because of how they regarded themselves.

Then Caleb (and I imagine Joshua) stood up before Moses and after seeing what the others had seen said;

> *Then Caleb quieted the people before Moses, and said, "Let us go up at once and take possession, for we are well able to overcome it." Numbers 13:30 NKJV*

He noted the giants were indeed real. Verse 33b is very revealing:

> *"...and we were like grasshoppers in our own sight, and so we were in their sight." Numbers 13:33b NKJV*

However Joshua and Caleb were convinced that with God on their side they would indeed be victorious.

The enemy will see you as you see yourself. Which leads us to Romans 12; we must renew our mind daily with the Word of God. The truth is we are all renewing our minds all day everyday but what with? In our world we have so much input, some good, some the opinions of others and some just rubbish. We must monitor what we are taking in!

> *And do not be conformed to this world, but be transformed by the renewing of your mind,*

so that you may prove what the will of God is, that which is good and acceptable and perfect.
Romans 12:2 NASB2020

We need to put on the new man, we are new creations in Him. We must begin to live like new creations. Read Romans 6:5-14 especially v6 knowing, v9 knowing, v11 consider.

*For if we have become united with Him in the likeness of His death, certainly we shall also be in the likeness of His resurrection, **knowing** this, that our old self was crucified with Him, in order that our body of sin might be done away with, so that we would no longer be slaves to sin; for the one who has died is freed from sin. Now if we have died with Christ, we believe that we shall also live with Him, **knowing** that Christ, having been raised from the dead, is never to die again; death no longer is master over Him. For the death that He died, He died to sin once for all time; but the life that He lives, He lives to God. So you too, **consider** yourselves to be dead to sin, but alive to God in Christ Jesus. Therefore sin is not to reign in your mortal body so that you obey its lusts, and do not go on presenting the parts of your body to sin as instruments of unrighteousness; but present yourselves to God as those who are alive from the dead, and your body's parts as instruments of righteousness for*

God. For sin shall not be master over you, for you are not under the Law but under grace.
Romans 6:5-14 NASB2020

When we are dead to sin we are alive in Christ. That is the reality of the 'new man'. Let me say it is not that we will never sin however, it will become less and less. The reason for that is our sin will become more offensive as we renew our minds - becoming more like Christ.

This leads us to the armour of God.

Finally, be strong in the Lord and in the strength of His might. Put on the full armor of God, so that you will be able to stand firm against the schemes of the devil. For our struggle is not against flesh and blood, but against the rulers, against the powers, against the world forces of this darkness, against the spiritual forces of wickedness in the heavenly places. Therefore, take up the full armor of God, so that you will be able to resist on the evil day, and having done everything, to stand firm. Stand firm therefore, having belted your waist with truth, and having put on the breastplate of righteousness, and having strapped on your feet the preparation of the gospel of peace; in addition to all, taking up the shield of faith with which you will be able to extinguish all the flaming arrows of the evil one. *And take the helmet of salvation and the sword of the Spirit, which is the word of God.* Ephesians 6:10-17 NASB2020

Paul admonishes us to be strong in the Lord and in the power of His might and put on the full armour of God, why? So that you will be able to stand firm against the schemes of the devil. Another very important point is that our struggle is not against flesh and blood, but against the rulers, against the powers, the forces of darkness in this world, against the spiritual forces of wickedness in the heavenly places or the spirit realm. This is what we must know in order to conquer the land that the Lord has promised.

Stand firm therefore having girded your loins with truth, wear the belt of truth, wrap it around your life.

Wear the belt of truth? Wrap it around your life?

So what does this mean for me today?

For me it means; let the truth of God's Word surround you and strengthen you. As we allow the Word to become flesh in us we are strengthened, we are protected. Remembering it is Jesus (the Word) who always causes us to triumph, we cannot do it on our own.

The Word of God is my foundation that must be

our confession because in that simple statement of Faith, we are strengthening our resolve in all situations. Which in turn leads to victory, triumph in all things as we stand firm!

Having put on the breastplate of righteousness.

This is so important and we can wear it because of the gift of righteousness (see Romans 5:17) that we have. Because of Jesus Christ - it is a gift - it is nothing we can earn. Praise God it is not dependant on us! I love that the righteousness of God protects my heart.

Having shod your feet with the preparation of the gospel of peace.

The Word which we all know is Jesus is the gospel of peace. Oh that we would walk in that revelation and seek peace and pursue it. We are called to be peacemakers and sometimes in order to accomplish that we must be peace breakers - breakers of false peace.

In addition to all, taking up the shield of Faith with which you will be able to extinguish all the fiery darts of the evil one.

When I talk to people they are always very quick to tell me they have great, huge faith which is excellent - I wonder then why are they being constantly beaten up by the enemy? This is not a criticism, it is an observation. I pray we would all have shields of faith that protect us from the crown of our head to the soles of our feet. However, I have seen many shields that resemble a handkerchief which you have to keep moving for protection. Faith comes by hearing and hearing by the Word of God!

And take the helmet of salvation.

It is very important to protect our mind. It reminds us that we have the mind of Jesus Christ. It reminds us who we are in Him and that is the authority we stand in, the authority we have over the enemy.

And the sword of the Spirit which is the Word of God!

In order to wield the Word with great skill we must first know the Word. There is a scripture I find most inspiring:

> *A warrior filled with wisdom ascends into the high place and releases breakthrough, bringing down the strongholds of the mighty. Proverbs 21:22* TPT

Back to Joshua - in Numbers when he and Caleb went in to spy out the land they didn't see the problem they saw the promise. They weren't blind to the giants but because of the promise they knew they could take them!

Then in Joshua 2 they come to spy out Jericho, a huge fortified city. They didn't actually conquer Jericho until Chapter 6. Why the delay? God gave them a strategy which they followed and brought down the walls of Jericho. They could have run in sooner as they did in Ai and run ahead of God, been completely out of His timing and got beaten up. But in the Jericho instance they followed the strategy. I love what the spies Joshua sent into Jericho said on their return in Joshua 2:24;

> *They said to Joshua, "Surely the Lord has given all the land into our hands; moreover, all the inhabitants the land have melted away before us." Joshua 2:24 NASB1995*

Don't see the problem - see the promise!

What God says is always bigger and more powerful.

Let's look at Luke 4, Jesus the 2nd Adam is in the wilderness being tempted by the devil. How does He nullify satan's attacks? With the Word - it is written! They were not simply words just as today they are not simply words. When we utter them I like to visualise the hosts of heaven catching them as they come out of my mouth and in an instant ushering them to hit their mark. That's our authority which Jesus gave us.

As You sent Me into the world, I also have sent

them into the world. John 17:18 NKJV

Jesus has commissioned us to a higher calling and He did not send us unarmed.

The glory which You have given Me I also have given to them, so that they may be one, just as We are one; I in them and You in Me, that they may be perfected in unity, so that the world may know that You sent Me, and You loved them, just as You loved Me. John 17:22-23 NASB2020

There are a couple of interesting points here:

1. Glory can be translated as honour or reputation so as we look at the reputation of Jesus, He carried the authority of the Father.
2. The other is Unity - as we get to that place of unity with each other the glory will be on us in the fullness of what that is.

Let's look at the following 2 verses in Luke.

Now He called the twelve together and gave them power and authority over all the demons, and the power to heal diseases. Luke 9:1 NASB2020

Behold, I have given you authority to tread on serpents and scorpions, and over all the power of the enemy, and nothing will injure you. Luke 10:19 NASB1995

We are His disciples and the Bible is a love letter written to us, therefore everything that has been already given we can access today. It is imperative that we know the Word and know it well so we never go out unarmed!

I discovered something just recently about when Jesus was on the cross and He said, "It is finished". This can also be translated as "It is accomplished" - the fulfilment of the promises given to Abram, Moses, Joshua, David and so on. Jesus accomplished! He didn't just finish it as that would be the end however accomplishment gives us an open door to move on and conquer!

An interesting side note is that it started in a garden with Eve and ended with Jesus coming out of the tomb to a woman called Mary.

It is important to know who you are fighting, who is your enemy? I hear a resounding the devil/satan, and whilst that is true it is only in part. Satan was a created being just like every other angel. What he is not is everything God is; he is not omnipotent, he is not omnipresent, he is not omniscient!

So what does that mean? He is not all powerful, he is not everywhere all at once and he is not all knowing. He is not GOD or anything close.

What he has developed is a network of demon

forces that can operate through human beings if the door is open and the welcome mat is laid out. In saying that we do not battle against flesh and blood but according to Ephesians 6:12;

> ....against the rulers, against the powers, against the world forces of this darkness, against the spiritual forces of wickedness in the heavenly places'. NASB2020

When you think about that for a moment it may seem overwhelming however now is the time to look at the promise and not the problem!

As we once again look at Joshua in chapter 3:9-10;

> Then Joshua said to the sons of Israel, "Come here, and hear the words of the LORD your God." Joshua said, "By this you shall know that the living God is among you, and that He will assuredly dispossess from before you the Canaanite, the Hittite, the Hivite, the Perizzite, the Girgashite, the Amorite, and the Jebusite." Joshua 3:9-10 NASB1995

In this section of the book we are going to unpack a little about these giants, principalities and demon forces. My hope in this is that we may very quickly recognise them in the world today and co-labouring with the Lord dispossess them as the scripture says.

Since the Hittites are spoken of in Joshua 1:4, I think it is prudent to begin there.

For God has not given us a spirit of fear, but of power and of love and of a sound mind.
2 Timothy 1:7 NKJV

CHAPTER 3

Occupying The Land

As a child of promise you have been promised victory, provision and blessing. You have been given a dream, destiny, wholeness and restoration of everything that the locust has eaten.

We have talked about claiming and conquering, now we must occupy the promises for ourselves and our children and then our grandchildren and great grandchildren - even great great grandchildren and so on.

We should always live like Jesus is coming back tomorrow and plan as though He isn't coming for a thousand years.

So an important part of occupying or possessing the land is forward planning, but we must plan with God's wisdom and strategy.

Occupying the promises speaks to me of the maturing of the saints. And as such we would be well practiced in the use of the weapons in our arsenal; able to hold off any attack of the enemy.

The enemy will try again.

And so when the devil had finished every temptation, he left Him until an opportune time. Luke 4:13 NASB2020

If that was his strategy with Jesus, it hasn't changed for us and he will try again usually when we least expect it.

Jesus has already won this victory, so we just stand in our full armour looking at the promise of God - our destiny - not the problem of this circumstance. (Refer to Chapter 2). It takes practice and that is why the unity of the brethren is incredibly important so we protect one another.

Mentorship is important for all of us. It is having someone who is further along the road who can proficiently guide us through the mine fields of life.

Whatever has been stolen must be returned. Jesus didn't leave any loose ends or any unfinished business.

The issue is never with the Lord, it is always with us. So there are always things to be tidied up.

CHAPTER 4

Giants In The Land

In this section I would like to address the issue of giants in the land.

What do the giants of the old testament look like today? Are they still around today? How do they operate in our world?

Because the bad guys don't always wear black hats like in cowboy movies, sometimes it may be more difficult to recognise them. My goal here is to remove the camouflage which has successfully hidden these entities for years. To bring the things of the darkness into the light of Jesus Christ.

None of this is exhaustive rather written to 'whet your appetite' for closer examination of these entities. I guess the main goal here is helping to reveal how these demon spirits manifest in today's world.

The most important key in all of this is asking for Holy Spirit who Jesus named as our 'helper' to help us. To enable us with the Holy Spirit Gift of Discerning of Spirits.

> *"I will ask the Father, and He will give you another Helper, so that He may be with you forever;"* John 14:16 NASB2020

> *"But the Helper, the Holy Spirit whom the Father will send in My name, He will teach you all things, and remind you of all that I said to you."* John 14:26 NASB2020

> *"When the Helper comes, whom I will send to you from the Father, namely, the Spirit of truth who comes from the Father, He will testify about Me,"* John 15:26 NASB2020

> *"But I tell you the truth: it is to your advantage that I am leaving; for if I do not leave, the Helper will not come to you; but if I go, I will send Him to you."* John 16:7 NASB2020

Now, let's look at this in Joshua;

> *Joshua told the Israelites, "Come closer and listen to the words of YAHWEH your God. This is how you will know for sure that the Living God is among you. As you advance into the land, he*

will drive out before you the Canaanites, Hittites, Hivites, Perizzites, Girgashites, Amorites, and Jebusites. Joshua 3:9-10 TPT

Wow! God said He was going to drive those giants out of the land - essentially the Israelites just had to turn up and BELIEVE.

Let's look at those giants. Their names will often give us clues as to who they are.

The Canaanites and the Amorites were the largest and most powerful tribes. The Canaanites dwelt in the lowlands whilst the Amorites resided in the high country.

The Hebrew word for Canaanites means 'those who traffic in materialism,' 'Merchants or pirates', they represent the love of money.

The Hebrew word for Amorites means 'those who live on high' or 'summit dwellers'; they represent pride and arrogance.

The Hebrew word for Hittites means 'those broken in pieces', 'Terror or dread'; represent anger and violence.

The Hebrew word for Hivites means 'life born without effort' or 'beastly life'; they represent human effort and reliance on self.

The Hebrew word for Perizzites means 'rustic', 'country dwellers' or 'backwoods'; they represent a lack of vision and initiative.

The Hebrew word for Girgashites means 'Dense, condensed marshy ground' representative of ignorance and an unwillingness to learn.

The Hebrew word for Jebusites means 'Trampled down under foot'. They represent fear and anxiety that cripple spiritual growth.

Jesus has empowered us to overcome and conquer these inner strongholds.

Unbelief, not giants defeated the children of Israel. Likewise today, unbelief not your problems or circumstances will defeat you - if you allow it.

I pray that this, with the Holy Spirit will help to identify and have victory over these things in our lives.

CHAPTER 5

The Hittites

The Hittites were the first giants mentioned that Joshua in his new role as leader encountered. We find this related in Joshua 1.

From the wilderness and this Lebanon, even as far as the great river, the river Euphrates, all the land of the Hittites, and as far as the Great Sea toward the setting of the sun will be your territory.
Joshua 1:4 NASB2020

Are the Hittites around today? Are they besetting us as they did in Joshua's day? Or is it simply historic and we don't need to bother about any of these giants?

The Hittites are the giant (principality perhaps) that seeks to and has the potential to paralyse us.

It is the spirit of fear, we must recognise it and

know how to deal with it.

It has been said fear is man's deadliest enemy. Fear has the potential to destroy man - spirit, soul and body. It is necessary for us to destroy this enemy which will make its home in our soul before it destroys us.

Fear is unreasonable, unfounded, persistent and tormenting. As such this thing has no place in a believer's life.

CHAPTER 6

The Amorites

One of the giants in the land is the Amorite spirit - this one is all about our words. Our own words born out of our pride and arrogance that gives an unrealistic superiority. So we can finally be in the land of promise and literally talk ourselves out of it.

Words have power, to occupy the land successfully we must put a watch over our mouths.

> *Do not trust in a friend; Do not put your confidence in a companion; Guard the doors of your mouth from her who lies in your bosom. Micah 7:5* NKJV

> *You are snared by the words of your mouth; You are taken by the words of your mouth.*

Proverbs 6:2 NKJV

*The tongue of the wise uses knowledge rightly,
But the mouth of fools pours forth foolishness.
Proverbs 15:2* NKJV

*Death and life are in the power of the tongue,
And those who love it will eat its fruit.
Proverbs 18:21* NKJV

There is great power in the words that we speak choose your words carefully.

And Jesus answered and said to them, "Have faith in God. Truly I say to you, whoever says to this mountain, 'Be taken up and thrown into the sea,' and does not doubt in his heart, but believes that what he says is going to happen, it will be granted to him. Therefore, I say to you, all things for which you pray and ask, believe that you have received them, and they will be granted to you". Mark 11:22-24 NASB2020

All things are all things! Sometimes we don't go for the all because of how we view ourselves.

All those scripture truths underline the power of good Godly words.

So how about this scripture in Proverbs?

From the fruit of a man's mouth he enjoys good,

But the desire of the treacherous is violence. The one who guards his mouth preserves his life; The one who opens wide his lips comes to ruin.
Proverbs 13:2-3 NASB1995

You will have what you say!

That is why we must be aware of and conquer this Amorite spirit. Our mouths were created to Praise God but the deception manifested in this spirit destroys our praise and derails our lives so we may find ourselves once again not living in the land of promise.

So let's stay close to the Lord and let Him guide us, protect us and admonish us - that we may dwell peacefully and securely in the land He has given us.

CHAPTER 7

The Canaanites

This spirit or principality is one that we are so familiar with. Most times we do not acknowledge that it is the enemy and not the Spirit of God behind it. This is due to who this giant is and how it manifests. It tells us we should have everything our heart desires. Greed is good and more is better. We can delude ourselves that when we have the more we will give more to the ministry or the poor. The truth is, if we are not giving from what we currently have we will not give when we have more. We will never have enough!

This spirit is often known as a trafficking spirit. Therefore it is at the forefront of commerce and trade. It is the spirit of greed and lust for material things. It is the bait that satan uses to successfully bring people down. It promises fulfilment and happiness but most often it delivers chaos and destruction.

We have all heard of people who have won huge amounts of money in lotteries only to be worse off a short time later.

Not just financially but it has the potential to destroy families.

In Joshua 7 we see the story of Achan who hid some gold, silver and beautiful garments in direct disobedience to God. It cost him and his family their lives.

Judas chose to betray Jesus for 30 pieces of silver. It did not bring him peace and joy. He later went out and hanged himself. Matthew 27:3-5.

Ananias and Sapphira chose to lie to the Holy Spirit about the sale of their property, they both paid with their lives.

The Canaanite spirit is subtle and operates in an imperceptible way wedging itself between man and God bringing despair and ruin to those who fall prey to it.

Let me be clear:

God is not against you having things. He is however against things having you!

If we seek after material things we are idolising them. We need to trust God and His goodness.

For the Gentiles eagerly seek all these things; for your heavenly Father knows that you need all these things. But seek first His kingdom and His righteousness, and all these things will be added to you. Matthew 6:32-33 NASB1995

CHAPTER 8

The Hivites

This giant is not as obvious in its manifestations as others we are looking at. That is of course the Hivite is a master of disguise. At its very core it is deception and its prime objective is to lure us into its claims of providing pleasure and prosperity. The fine print says that you will pay with your life (but who reads the fine print these days?)

It comes to us portraying the world full of illusions, delusions and other dubious delights as fulfilling life, an environment that satisfies the soul. Today young people are extremely vulnerable to this spirit and very easily fall prey to its bright lights and empty promises which lead to death. These promises are everything that are attractive to natural man. However, in the cold light of day, when the lights and the music are turned off, when the alcohol and or drugs have worn off. Or perhaps when the sex is over they may begin to see this isn't life, it's a lie and there is a price to pay.

It is important to remember anyone whether a Christian or not can fall prey to this voracious enemy. Be on guard!

Scripture has this to say in John;

> *"The one who loves his life loses it, and the one who hates his life in this world will keep it to eternal life." John 12:25 NASB2020*

> *Do not love the world nor the things in the world. If anyone loves the world, the love of the Father is not in him. 1 John 2:15 NASB2020*

Whilst the Hivite spirit was in play in the life of the prodigal son, it is rarely as obvious. (Look up Luke 15:11-32)

The story in Genesis 34 about Dinah (Jacob's daughter) looked innocent enough but led to her seduction and rape. In Joshua 9 the Gibeonites deceived the Israelites. The important note for me in that story was Israel did not take the counsel of the Lord. (See verse 14.) I would recommend you read those accounts in the Bible.

> *There is a way which seems right to a man, But its end is the way of death.*

Proverbs 14:12 NASB1995

We need to take the counsel of the Lord even when things look ok. Always remember it's ok to say NO! We don't have to go places or do things simply because we're asked to.

How do we overcome this spirit?

Receive the Grace of God!

For the grace of God has appeared, bringing salvation to all people, instructing us to deny ungodliness and worldly desires and to live sensibly, righteously, and in a godly manner in the present age, looking for the blessed hope and the appearing of the glory of our great God and Savior, Christ Jesus... Titus 2:11-13 NASB2020

If indeed you have tasted that the Lord is gracious. 1 Peter 2:3 NKJV

For by grace you have been saved through faith; and this is not of yourselves, it is the gift of God Ephesians 2:8 NASB2020

Live in the Word of God!

When you live in the truth it is not easy to be deceived

I have written to you, fathers, because you know Him who has been from the beginning. I have written to you, young men, because you are strong, and the word of God remains in you, and you have overcome the evil one.
1 John 2:14 NASB2020

In Luke 4, Jesus answers the devil with.... "It is written" three times (v4, v8 v12).

So Jesus was saying to those Jews who had believed Him, "If you continue in My word, then you are truly My disciples; and you will know the truth, and the truth will set you free." John 8:31-32 NASB2020

Get a revelation of God!

A revelation of God/Jesus Christ will change you. Just one touch of heaven and you will never be the same.

In the first part of Isaiah 6, Isaiah received a revelation of God and His glory.

Isaiah bemoans his human frailty as he gets that revelation of the awesomeness of God.

Paul in 2 Corinthians 12 experienced revelations and visions which strengthened him to withstand the world's temptations.

Recognise we are citizens of heaven!

Hebrews 11 states and restates the great heroes of faith who had their eyes firmly fixed on their home in heaven. That amazing city John describes in Revelation 21 - that is our home! We are strangers and pilgrims on this earth. Why? Because our true citizenship is in Heaven. Therefore we are charged to live as ambassadors representing Heaven and our King. If we firmly grasp this it will change our posture and crystallise our purpose.

Fall in love with Jesus!

When we truly have that love relationship with Christ - which like any love relationship should grow and deepen every day - that will protect us from the lure of satan as nothing else can.

Read the Word - Jesus is the Word! I often say the Bible is a love letter written personally by Holy Spirit at God's behest to us. Meditate on it, wash yourself in it and let Holy Spirit take it deep within you. Ask the Lord to give you a revelation of His great love for you.

These keys will help you to discern that even though it sparkles and glitters, it is completely worthless.

CHAPTER 9

The Girgashites

This spirit is often characterised as the one that leads believers into a backslidden state. That is of course true and yet it may over simplify the depths of that state.

The children of Israel as we know wandered the wilderness because of their unbelief. These were those who had seen and experienced the great and mighty power of God. They had the promise of His Word, that He had given them the land of Canaan and they only had to go in and possess it. However, having tasted the fruit of the promised land and experienced the mighty works of God, they turned back to Egypt and discussed the appointment of a new leader to take them. You can read this in Numbers 13:17-14:5.

We can read this incredulous at their decision to return to their captivity. Egypt was the land of their harsh captivity and cruel slavery. A place where children were snatched from their mothers and then brutally murdered (Exodus 1). We can shake our heads astonished as they turned away from the promised land back to Egypt.

Behind this was the Girgashite giant recognised as the turning back spirit. It is sinister and subtle and at work today.

This is more than missing a couple of church meetings, it is a complete turning away from Christ and returning to the dark side.

This giant will stand against when we are vulnerable. Firstly when we are new believers and have not yet fully embraced and experienced the person and the presence of Christ.

To illustrate this I was teaching in a new believers course and a young man approached me after the lesson. He explained he was having great difficulty hanging on to faith when everything in his life was going from bad to worse in the natural. He had been in business and financially successful, in his words he was living the dream - house cars and plenty of cash. Then he made a decision for Christ and almost overnight everything he had put his faith in (business, cars, houses, cash) had one way or another been taken from him. It had been discovered that his business partner had been dealing very dishonestly and things collapsed like a house of cards.

He was looking back to the lifestyle of comfort and luxury ignoring the dishonest and possibly criminal behaviour of his associate. He seriously did not believe he could endure a Christian life if all he had in his future was lack and hardship.

At this point I was earnestly seeking the Holy Spirit for wisdom. What I remember saying to him was these things were temporal however, the Love of God is eternal and He always desires the best for us and sometimes our desires and His don't match up. The more we get to know Jesus and fall in love with Him, we will start to see things from His perspective and our desires will match up. What the Christian life does promise us is life more abundant, life to the fullest. The peace and joy the Lord ensures is priceless as is the divine promise of eternal life with the Lord.

I am pleased to say thirty years on he is a mature Christian living his life for God's glory.

Matthew 24:12 warns us 'in the last days the love of many will wax cold'.

So now we are addressing mature believers. Many of whom have overcome many things but perhaps the excitement or gloss has gone off their walk. This is always because the sinister presence of the Girgashite is lurking there.

Sometimes people's pride and 'spiritual superiority' will convince them they are disciplined in the Christian life. They think they have it all together and are so in control they need not pursue Christian disciplines anymore.

This is indeed a dangerous practice!

There are others in this group who are bolstering the ranks of those fascinated with the occult, astrology and so on.

Chasing after the 'supernatural' forgetting that because of Christ we already are.

There are other examples of this in scripture. Demas left Paul in 2 Timothy 4:10 having experienced the power of God many times through Paul's ministry.

> *'for Demas has forsaken me, having loved this present world, and has departed for Thessalonica....' 2 Timothy 4:10* NKJV

And of course;

> *'remember Lot's wife' Luke 17:32* NASB2020

She didn't want to leave the comfort of her life

ignoring the stench of sin.

When things are challenging please ignore the urging of the Girgashite to turn back. Look again to Jesus - our love relationship with Christ is the antidote.

CHAPTER 10

The Perizzites

The literal meaning of Perizzites is unwalled town or village. In the Bible we note the custom of cities flourishing behind great walls.

A city without walls was an invitation to the enemy to enter at will.

> *Like a city that is broken into and without walls So is a person who has no self-control over his spirit.* Proverbs 25:28 NASB2020

Not all defences need to be stone walls.

The root word Perizzite is derived from means to separate.

So it would follow that without protection separation from God is not too difficult. It is easy to overrun a city or town without walls, then the inhabitants can be bent to another's will.

In God we have impenetrable protection. He's our rock, our fortress, strong tower, hiding place, shield, shelter and refuge.

> *He said, "The LORD is my rock and my fortress and my deliverer; My God, my rock, in whom I take refuge, My shield and the horn of my salvation, my stronghold and my refuge; My savior, You save me from violence." 2 Samuel 22:2-3 NASB2020*

> *"I love You, O Lord, my strength." The Lord is my rock and my fortress and my deliverer, My God, my rock, in whom I take refuge; My shield and the horn of my salvation, my stronghold. I call upon the Lord, who is worthy to be praised, And I am saved from my enemies. Psalms 18:1-3 NASB1995*

> *My faithfulness and my fortress, My stronghold and my savior, My shield and He in whom I take refuge, Who subdues my people under me. Psalms 144:2 NASB2020*

God is our safe place - He is the place we fight from.

The battle against satan has already been won. Jesus did that, so our victory is ensured. So fight! The Lord has given us the victory. It is the fight of Faith in the Spirit Realm not the natural realm.

We have an important part to play in this, dispossessing the current occupants. We must consider our posture in this. Are we operating under stress and anxiety hoping for the best yet expecting the worse? Or is our posture that of the Sons of God? Seated in heavenly places with Jesus, so we operate from a place of rest.

One of the greatest keys in Spiritual Warfare is the Armour of God!

It is important to know and understand every component.

Loins Girded with Truth

How many have wondered what that actually means today. Our loins are our core which represent our strength. If our core is weak then we are weakened against attack. So what this is doing is wrapping our own spiritual strength with the Truth of God. Therefore fortifying ourselves against attacks of the enemy. So as we cover ourselves, wrap ourselves with the righteousness of God, His Divine Truth and perfect Holiness, we are completely protected from spiritual onslaught.

The Word of God must cover us - we must be secure in the Rhema Word not relying on our feelings or experiences.

Breastplate of Righteousness

In our world we could regard this as a bullet proof vest. It covers our heart. We know by Faith we have received the Gift of Righteousness.

> *For if by the offense of the one, death reigned through the one, much more will those who receive the abundance of grace and of the gift of righteousness reign in life through the One, Jesus Christ. Roman 5:17* NASB2020

This breastplate and the righteousness it represents brings Romans 8:1 to life in a very real way.

> *Therefore there is now no condemnation at all for those who are in Christ Jesus. Romans 8:1* NASB2020

We no longer have to endure the buffeting of the enemy through condemnation and accusation. Our conscience is clear and our hearts are stilled in that knowledge.

Feet are Shod with the Gospel of Peace

As believers how our feet are covered is incredibly important to our spiritual well being. It is the Gospel (the Good News) of Jesus Christ that is our firm foundation which brings the sense of peace to our lives as believers.

Peace is an irresistible force. As we walk in peace we raise a huge barrier of strength and protection against the enemy.

When our feet are shod with the gospel of peace we can live in peace. The peace of God will permeate every area of our lives.

The Shield of Faith

The scripture in Ephesians 6:16 reads;

Above all, taking the shield of faith with which you will be able to quench all the fiery darts of the wicked one. NKJV

That would suggest that whilst all the other components of our armour are important, Faith is over all. Nothing in God works without us having Faith in Him. So I would suggest that none of the other parts of the armour function without Faith. It is fundamental in our spiritual warfare.

CHAPTER 11

The Jebusites

This giant is left until last deliberately. It always seems to me when all the previous giants have done their worst and been defeated this one has been waiting with its vile bag of tricks.

We know Jerusalem is deemed as the Holy City of God. However, today as in the Bible it has the Jebusite as a squatter. That is one of the things we should recognise about this spirit - it will assume a place where it should not be. Therefore assuming the authority of that place.

Jerusalem is set aside as that place of divine sanctification where we can enjoy the heavenly promises.

As we look at the Jebusite in scripture the one that always springs to mind is Elijah and Jezebel.

The Jebusite was in Jerusalem when Nehemiah was called by God to rebuild the walls. The Jebusite was also in Jerusalem as David came to recapture the city.

It can just as easily assume place in our lives. Our ministries, our homes and families, our workplaces and so on. Ready and able to unleash it's vile manifestations upon the believers today.

I see something interesting as we look at the story of Elijah and the prophets of baal.

In 1 Kings 18, God caused Elijah to have a great victory over the 400 baal prophets. We all know how euphoric it is when we have great things happen in God. He was elated.

Then a word from Jezebel in 1 Kings 19:2;

> *Then Jezebel sent a messenger to Elijah, saying, "So may the gods do to me and even more, if I do not make your life as the life of one of them by tomorrow about this time." 1 Kings 19:2* NASB1995

Then scripture records something unthinkable.

> *And he was afraid and arose and ran for his life... 1 Kings 19:3a* NASB1995

It is important to read this portion of scripture.

Even though Elijah had just had the most extraordinary victory over the enemy's realm, one word from Jezebel caused him to run for his life.

As an aside; I just want to thank God for Holy Spirit who is here with us - Elijah did not have that comfort. I say that to remind us we don't have to run.

When that voice of discouragement comes to us and it will, we must run into our safe place - our strong tower.

In Nehemiah 4, when this same giant tried to discourage Nehemiah and the workers we see in verse 9;

But we prayed to our God

And God gave them a strategy!

But we prayed to our God, and because of them we set up a guard against them day and night. Nehemiah 4:9 NASB1995

In my Bible in Nehemiah before verse 9 the heading is DISCOURAGEMENT OVERCOME.

There it is - amazing! Pray to overcome discouragement.

Discouragement is the gateway, the subtle entrance for the Jebusite's unholy trinity - accusation, intimidation and manipulation. When discouragement opens the door it is very easy for the others to move on in.

Although Jezebel threatened Elijah's life; most times the desired result for the Jebusite is the sidelining of the man or woman of God. It causes them to doubt the vision and listen to the lie. If the Girgashite is around they may completely fall away.

That is not our future! Our destiny is in God. It is smart to know your enemy as he is unlikely to give you a free pass because you plead ignorance. He simply sees you as easy prey, low hanging fruit if you like. Embrace the body of Christ, there is the protection from so many of these giants as we come together.

When one is weak another is strong!

CHAPTER 12

The Last Word

I pray this is inspirational and encouraging. We can take back what the enemy has stolen and step into that which God predestined for us.

I encourage you to always look for the good.

Paul encourages the Philippians like this;

> *Finally, brethren, whatever is true, whatever is honorable, whatever is right, whatever is pure, whatever is lovely, whatever is of good repute, if there is any excellence and if anything worthy of praise, dwell on these things. The things you have learned and received and heard and seen in me, practice these things, and the God of peace will be with you.* Philippians 4:8-9 NASB1995

Amen.

The question for us as we face our mountain sometimes in the valley of indecision - do I face down this thing or do I enjoy my quiet unremarkable life? The answer is of course the same - they are simply there and they are not moving of their own volition. As we progress through this journey you will find you have the authority to command them to move. It is entirely our call which challenge we conquer and which we simply tolerate.

This book is offered to inspire, challenge, provoke and bless each and everyone whose hands it comes into. This has been a lifetime of discovery of 'What is this thing called Love?'

In fact there are different kinds of Love which will all bring a different harvest however that is another revelation.

So which seed have I planted?

Is it the seed for my desired harvest?

Faith is perhaps the simplest and most difficult discipline we ever have to master. I love that old saying, "from little acorns great oak trees grow". Those acorns are a metaphorical representation of our seed of faith. From those humble seed beginnings we grow and become all that we can be in God.

This is written to inspire and encourage.

The Seed of Faith…. it is in you!

www.theseedoffaithbook.com

ABOUT THE AUTHOR

Pamela Segneri is the co-founder of Integrity Restoration Ministries Inc and the co-founder and Host of firestartersTV. Her desire is to see you fulfil your God given destiny.

www.integritygroup.org.au

www.firestartersTV.com.au

www.ingramcontent.com/pod-product-compliance
Lightning Source LLC
Chambersburg PA
CBHW071833290426
44109CB00017B/1810